I·N·S·I·D·E DK G·U·I·D·E·S

AMAZING BUGS

Written by

MIRANDA MACQUITTY

Bluebottle
feeding on the
remains of
food on a fork

A DK PUBLISHING BOOK

Bees returning
to their hive

Editor Kitty Blount

Art editor Cormac Jordan

Senior art editor Diane Klein

Managing editor Gillian Denton

Managing art editor Julia Harris

Editorial consultant Steven Brooks

US Editor Camela Decaire

Picture research Sam Ruston

Production Charlotte Traill

Photography Andy Crawford, Geoff Brightling
Modelmakers Peter Minister, Gary Staab,
Chris Reynolds and the team at BBC Visual Effects

First American Edition, 1996
2 4 6 8 10 9 7 5 3 1

Published in the United States by DK Publishing, Inc.,
95 Madison Avenue
New York, New York 10016
Copyright © 1996 Dorling Kindersley Limited, London
Visit us on the World Wide Web at
http://www.dk.com

Dissected body
of a shieldbug

Mosquito feeding
on human blood

A CIP catalog record is available from the Library of Congress.
ISBN 0–7894–1010–9

Reproduced in Italy by G.R.B. Graphica, Verona
Printed in Singapore by Toppan

Cave-dwelling cricket

Magnified images
of a fruit fly
maggot

A mosquito's
mouthparts

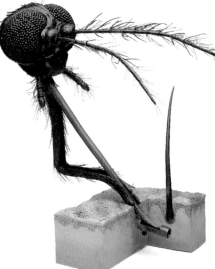

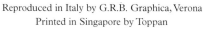

Contents

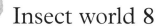

Model of wasp
showing flight
muscles

Cat flea

Voracious desert locust

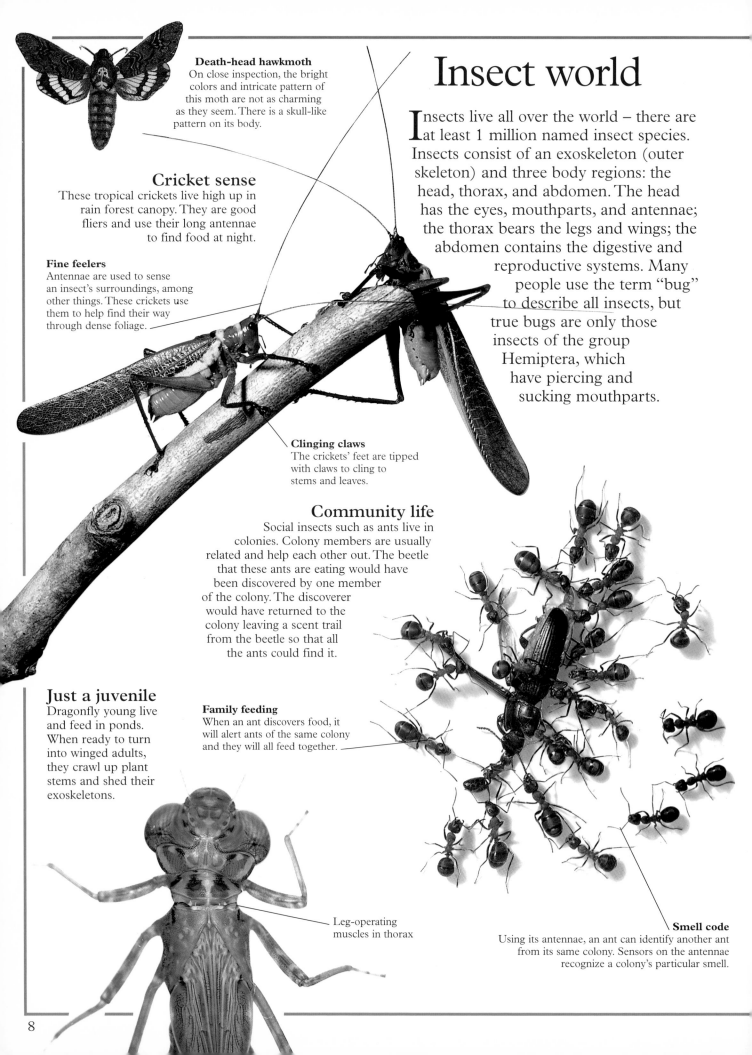

Death-head hawkmoth
On close inspection, the bright colors and intricate pattern of this moth are not as charming as they seem. There is a skull-like pattern on its body.

Insect world

Insects live all over the world – there are at least 1 million named insect species. Insects consist of an exoskeleton (outer skeleton) and three body regions: the head, thorax, and abdomen. The head has the eyes, mouthparts, and antennae; the thorax bears the legs and wings; the abdomen contains the digestive and reproductive systems. Many people use the term "bug" to describe all insects, but true bugs are only those insects of the group Hemiptera, which have piercing and sucking mouthparts.

Cricket sense
These tropical crickets live high up in rain forest canopy. They are good fliers and use their long antennae to find food at night.

Fine feelers
Antennae are used to sense an insect's surroundings, among other things. These crickets use them to help find their way through dense foliage.

Clinging claws
The crickets' feet are tipped with claws to cling to stems and leaves.

Community life
Social insects such as ants live in colonies. Colony members are usually related and help each other out. The beetle that these ants are eating would have been discovered by one member of the colony. The discoverer would have returned to the colony leaving a scent trail from the beetle so that all the ants could find it.

Just a juvenile
Dragonfly young live and feed in ponds. When ready to turn into winged adults, they crawl up plant stems and shed their exoskeletons.

Family feeding
When an ant discovers food, it will alert ants of the same colony and they will all feed together.

Leg-operating muscles in thorax

Smell code
Using its antennae, an ant can identify another ant from its same colony. Sensors on the antennae recognize a colony's particular smell.

Among the giants

Goliath beetles, found in the African tropics, are among the heaviest insects in the world. Males weigh over 3.5 oz (100 gm), about as much as a small apple. Despite their weight, goliath beetles can fly.

Covered for life
A beetle in its adult stage will not molt its large, protective exoskeleton.

Wing case

Red for danger!

Ladybugs are beetles; most have bright red, orange, or yellow wing cases (outer wings) to warn predators they taste nasty. Ladybugs prefer cold weather, and huddle together in cracks among rocks and on trees to stay warm. In places with hot, dry summers, they will fly to cooler elevations until the heat is past. Ladybugs eat aphids, among other plant-eating bugs, so gardeners are always happy to see them!

Frost resistant
Ladybugs can tolerate cold conditions and even frost.

Noxious knees
Ladybugs' knees produce a bad-smelling fluid, deterring predators.

Hard cover

Almost half of all the known species of insects are beetles. This jewel beetle's tough wing cases protect its delicate inner wings as it scurries around.

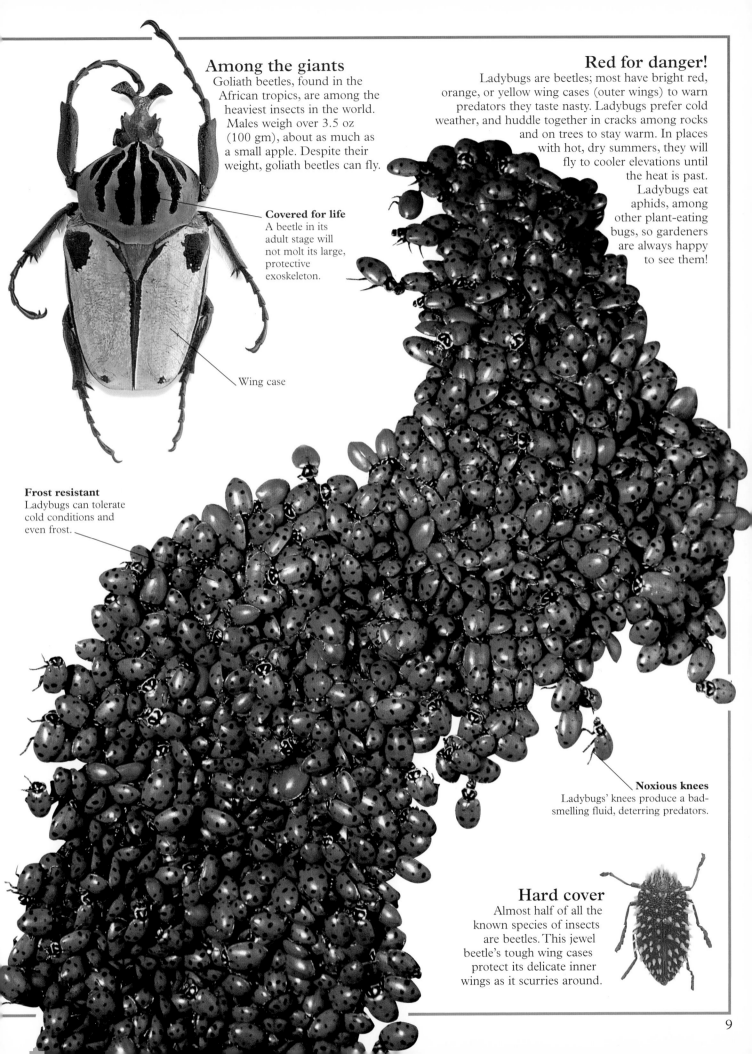

Outside an insect

The rhinoceros beetle has spikes on its body for wrestling with other males.

An insect's skeleton, called an exoskeleton, is on the outside, protecting the insect like a suit of armor. The exoskeleton covers the entire body, forming thick, protective plates, delicate wings, hairs, and even the eyes' transparent lenses. The exoskeleton is tough, and made mainly of a horny substance called chitin. The outermost layer is waxy to keep in body moisture. The exoskeleton must be molted for an insect to grow. Before it is molted, it becomes thinner as the insect absorbs all the nutrients from it. The old exoskeleton then splits, and the next stage emerges with a new exoskeleton. Before this hardens, the insect increases its size by swallowing air or water.

Careful coronet
During the day, the coronet moth rests on the bark of a tree. The moth's mottled colors are good camouflage, so it is unlikely to be spotted by predators.

Abdomen
Between each segment of the abdomen is a ring of thinner, more flexible exoskeleton. This allows the abdomen to bend.

Flaps for flying
The wings of insects are just thin extensions of the exoskeleton. Unlike birds, pterodactyls, and bats, insects did not convert an existing pair of limbs when they evolved wings. So this moth still has three pairs of legs as well as wings.

Landing platform
This petal looks like a female bumblebee's abdomen.

Eye spots
These may fool a predator into thinking the moth is a larger animal.

Shieldbug
The body of a shieldbug is wide and flat. Shieldbugs produce off-putting smells to warn attackers away, so they are also known as stinkbugs. The smells are produced by glands in the thorax. In some cases, the scent is strong enough to give a person a headache. This shieldbug's colors are produced by pigments in the exoskeleton. Some bugs are also iridescent (shiny) due to rays of light being bounced off microscopic layers within the exoskeleton.

Like a bee
The flowers of the bee orchid look like female bumblebees and attract male bumblebees. In attempting to mate with the flower, a male collects pollen on his body. When the frustrated bee attempts to mate with another bee orchid, he pollinates the flower.

Wing scales
The overlapping scales on the wings of a male morpho butterfly, found in South American rain forests, are a brilliant iridescent blue color. This is produced by light bouncing back from microscopic ridges on the surface and layers within the scales.

Back wing
Here, one of the shieldbug's back wings is stretched out to show it is like a delicate membrane. At rest, the back wings are folded over each other beneath the front wings.

Jaws on the outside
Insects' mouthparts are attached to the outside of the mouth. Those that chew their food have strong jaws that cut up food before it goes into the mouth, like this bush cricket.

Head gear
The spike on the bush cricket's head may make it awkward for predators trying to eat it.

Jaw

Upper lip

Lower lip

Sense receptors
There are many different kinds of sense receptors on the surface of the antennae.

Thick plate
In the shieldbug, a thick plate covers the first and some of the second segment of the thorax.

Hard head
The head capsule protects the brain and has attachments for the muscles that work the mouthparts and antennae.

Beak
The beak is used for sucking up food and is usually held underneath the body. The outer segmented part of the beak protects the piercing and sucking parts.

Thorax
The thorax is made of three segments. The first one carries the first pair of legs. The second and third each carry a pair of legs and wings.

Antennae
The exoskeleton covers all the segments of the antennae.

Coxa

Claws, on end of tarsus

One of six
Insects have six legs. Each one has five main parts.

Trochanter

Thick, protective wing base

Femur

Tarsus, divided into segments

Tibia

Antenna

Half wing
Each of the shieldbug's front pair of wings is divided into a thick, protective base, and a thin, membranous tip.

Thin, membranous wing tip

Extended head capsule

Keeping watch
Mantises have large eyes and good vision, and can swivel their heads, getting the best view of approaching prey. Mantises often sway from side to side. This allows them to judge distances, and tell when prey is within reach.

Thorax

Sitting pretty
An orchid mantis lies in wait for its prey. It blends in perfectly with the flower, making it hard for bees, or other insects visiting the flower, to see it.

Inside an insect

Inside an insect's exoskeleton are its soft body organs. The gut is a long tube in which food is digested and from which it is absorbed into the blood. The blood then carries the food to all the insect's tissues and organs. The blood is pumped around the body by the tube-shaped heart, which is helped by body movements. Waste is removed from the blood by the malpighian tubules, which act similarly to human kidneys. Solid waste collects at the end of the gut and is passed out through the anus. Unlike humans, insects do not have lungs and their blood does not carry oxygen. Instead they breathe through tracheae (pp. 18–19). The insect's actions are controlled by a brain and nerve cord.

Skeleton section
An insect exoskeleton is composed of layers that are produced by an inner sheet of cells.

Diaphragm
This membrane, the diaphragm, supports the heart. It also separates the heart from the blood-filled space that contains the body organs.

Anus, through which waste is excreted

Hindgut with thin lining

Malpighian tubules

Nerve center
Nerve centers are attached to the nerve cord. They send messages to muscles.

Digestive system
An insect's digestive system, as shown in this model of a locust, divides into three parts: the foregut, from mouth to gizzard; the midgut, from caecae to malpighian tubules; and the hindgut. Swallowed plant material is stored in the crop, in the foregut. From here it passes through the gizzard and into the midgut, where enzymes break it down for absorption into the bloodstream. The malpighian tubules absorb waste from the blood here, and this, along with solid food waste, passes into the hindgut. Water and salts are absorbed from these wastes, and the rectum then channels all the waste to the anus.

All aglow
Certain kinds of beetles, such as this click beetle, signal to their mates by giving out flashes of light. The flashes are produced by chemical reactions inside the body. Different species living in the same place use a particular number of flashes to avoid attracting the wrong mate.

X-ray bug
People get X-rays to show the state of their bones. Because insects' skeletons are on the outside, X-rays are used to reveal their tissues. This X-ray of a cockchafer beetle shows the outline of its jointed legs and its fan-shaped antennae.

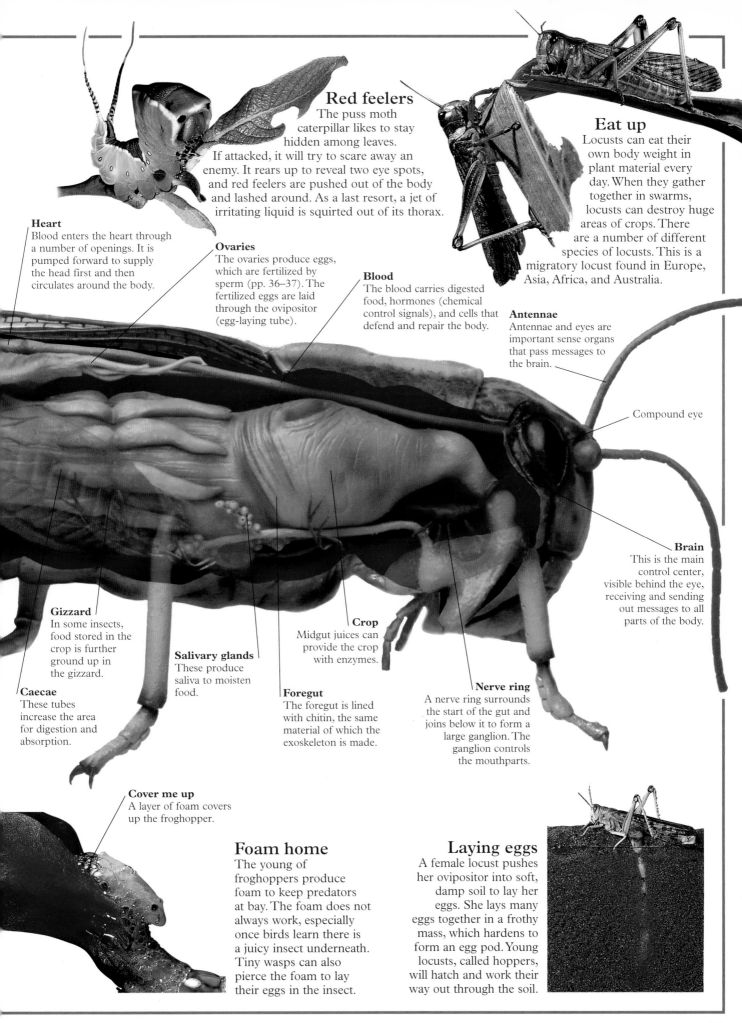

Red feelers
The puss moth caterpillar likes to stay hidden among leaves. If attacked, it will try to scare away an enemy. It rears up to reveal two eye spots, and red feelers are pushed out of the body and lashed around. As a last resort, a jet of irritating liquid is squirted out of its thorax.

Eat up
Locusts can eat their own body weight in plant material every day. When they gather together in swarms, locusts can destroy huge areas of crops. There are a number of different species of locusts. This is a migratory locust found in Europe, Asia, Africa, and Australia.

Heart
Blood enters the heart through a number of openings. It is pumped forward to supply the head first and then circulates around the body.

Ovaries
The ovaries produce eggs, which are fertilized by sperm (pp. 36–37). The fertilized eggs are laid through the ovipositor (egg-laying tube).

Blood
The blood carries digested food, hormones (chemical control signals), and cells that defend and repair the body.

Antennae
Antennae and eyes are important sense organs that pass messages to the brain.

Compound eye

Brain
This is the main control center, visible behind the eye, receiving and sending out messages to all parts of the body.

Gizzard
In some insects, food stored in the crop is further ground up in the gizzard.

Caecae
These tubes increase the area for digestion and absorption.

Salivary glands
These produce saliva to moisten food.

Crop
Midgut juices can provide the crop with enzymes.

Foregut
The foregut is lined with chitin, the same material of which the exoskeleton is made.

Nerve ring
A nerve ring surrounds the start of the gut and joins below it to form a large ganglion. The ganglion controls the mouthparts.

Cover me up
A layer of foam covers up the froghopper.

Foam home
The young of froghoppers produce foam to keep predators at bay. The foam does not always work, especially once birds learn there is a juicy insect underneath. Tiny wasps can also pierce the foam to lay their eggs in the insect.

Laying eggs
A female locust pushes her ovipositor into soft, damp soil to lay her eggs. She lays many eggs together in a frothy mass, which hardens to form an egg pod. Young locusts, called hoppers, will hatch and work their way out through the soil.

Bloodsucker

Mosquitoes use their needlelike mouthparts to pierce human skin and then to suck blood. The itchy "bite" is a reaction to a mixture of substances they inject into the blood before sucking it. This mixture makes the blood flow more strongly and stops it from clotting. Only female mosquitoes suck blood, which provides them with protein to help develop their eggs. Male mosquitoes take sips of sugary fluids, such as nectar. A female mosquito homes in on a human by sensing carbon dioxide, exhaled in breath. When she lands, her mouthparts probe the skin for a blood capillary. Certain kinds of female mosquitoes can be deadly because they pass a disease onto their hosts. The disease, malaria, is caused by a microscopic parasite and kills up to 2 million people a year. The parasite is picked up when the mosquito feeds on the blood of an infected person. It is passed on as she injects saliva into another person. Other blood-sucking insects, such as tsetse flies, can also transmit diseases.

Male mosquito
Unlike the female mosquito, the male mosquito does not suck blood.

Nasty disease
This kissing bug's "bite" transmits a nasty disease in addition to leaving an itchy swelling.

Kissing bug
This tropical American bug is called a kissing bug because it "bites" people's faces. It carries the parasite that causes a fever called Chagas' disease. The parasite is passed in the bug's droppings immediately after it has fed on blood. A person scratching the bite then introduces the parasite into the wound.

Sap suckers
Aphids suck sap from plants. Their mouthparts pierce a leaf surface and a tube is thrust inside. Sap-digesting saliva is carried into the leaf and digested sap is then sucked up.

Food canal
Blood is sucked up through this canal into the mosquito.

Mandible
The sharp points of the mandibles break the surface of the host's skin.

Protective sheath

Bad bite
Blackflies feed off both people and livestock. Plagues of blackflies can kill cattle and horses by poisoning their blood.

Hypopharynx
The salivary duct runs down the hypopharynx, carrying substances that encourage the blood to flow.

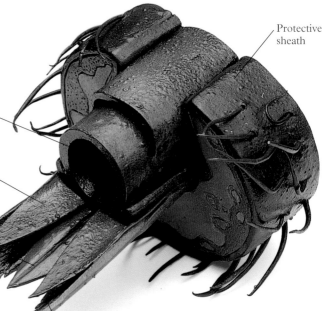

Maxilla
The serrated edges cut through the skin.

Mouthparts
When not in use, a mosquito's piercing and sucking mouthparts are held safe within a protective sheath. The piercing mandibles and maxillae are sometimes called the "stylets."

Not just us
There are more than 3,000 kinds of mosquitoes. The females of most varieties suck blood. Besides humans, mosquitoes feed on everything from rabbits and cattle to birds and snakes. Even mudskipper fish can fall prey to mosquitoes.

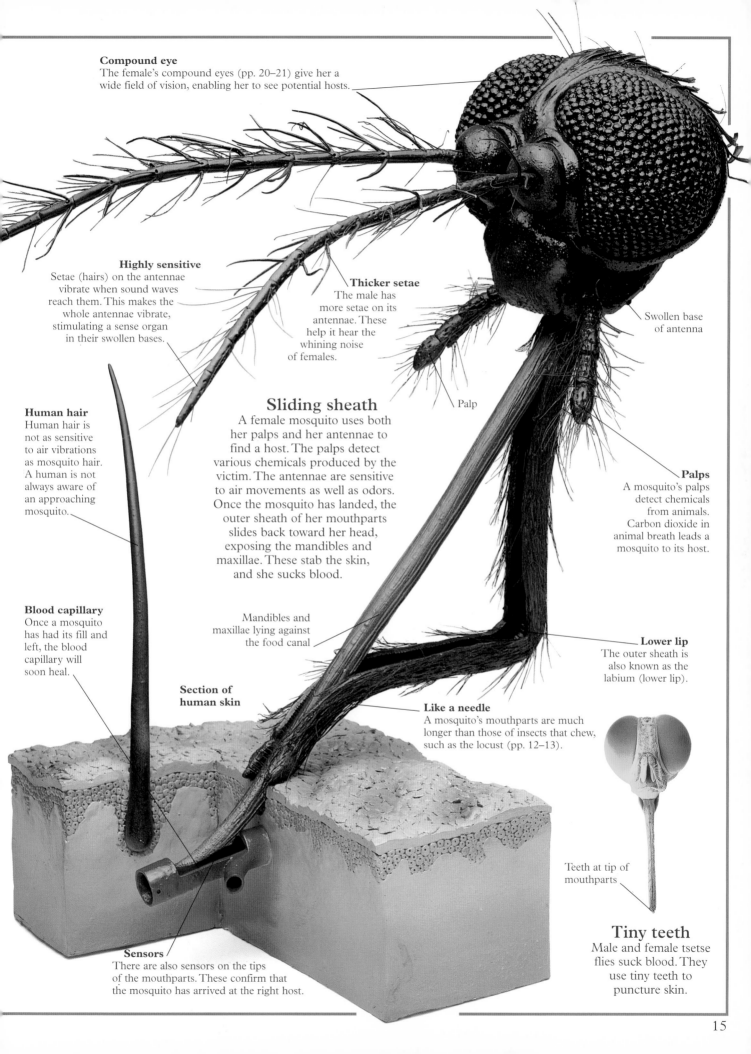

Compound eye
The female's compound eyes (pp. 20–21) give her a wide field of vision, enabling her to see potential hosts.

Highly sensitive
Setae (hairs) on the antennae vibrate when sound waves reach them. This makes the whole antennae vibrate, stimulating a sense organ in their swollen bases.

Thicker setae
The male has more setae on its antennae. These help it hear the whining noise of females.

Human hair
Human hair is not as sensitive to air vibrations as mosquito hair. A human is not always aware of an approaching mosquito.

Sliding sheath
A female mosquito uses both her palps and her antennae to find a host. The palps detect various chemicals produced by the victim. The antennae are sensitive to air movements as well as odors. Once the mosquito has landed, the outer sheath of her mouthparts slides back toward her head, exposing the mandibles and maxillae. These stab the skin, and she sucks blood.

Swollen base of antenna

Palp

Palps
A mosquito's palps detect chemicals from animals. Carbon dioxide in animal breath leads a mosquito to its host.

Blood capillary
Once a mosquito has had its fill and left, the blood capillary will soon heal.

Mandibles and maxillae lying against the food canal

Section of human skin

Lower lip
The outer sheath is also known as the labium (lower lip).

Like a needle
A mosquito's mouthparts are much longer than those of insects that chew, such as the locust (pp. 12–13).

Teeth at tip of mouthparts

Sensors
There are also sensors on the tips of the mouthparts. These confirm that the mosquito has arrived at the right host.

Tiny teeth
Male and female tsetse flies suck blood. They use tiny teeth to puncture skin.

Sponger

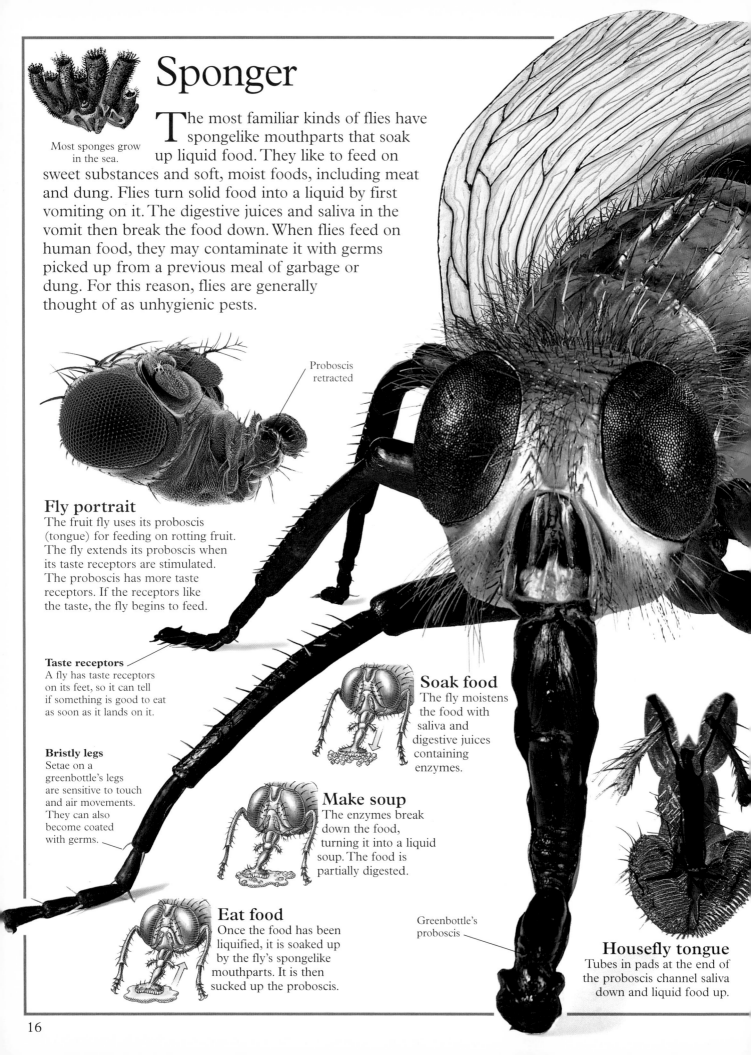

The most familiar kinds of flies have spongelike mouthparts that soak up liquid food. They like to feed on sweet substances and soft, moist foods, including meat and dung. Flies turn solid food into a liquid by first vomiting on it. The digestive juices and saliva in the vomit then break the food down. When flies feed on human food, they may contaminate it with germs picked up from a previous meal of garbage or dung. For this reason, flies are generally thought of as unhygienic pests.

Most sponges grow in the sea.

Proboscis retracted

Fly portrait
The fruit fly uses its proboscis (tongue) for feeding on rotting fruit. The fly extends its proboscis when its taste receptors are stimulated. The proboscis has more taste receptors. If the receptors like the taste, the fly begins to feed.

Taste receptors
A fly has taste receptors on its feet, so it can tell if something is good to eat as soon as it lands on it.

Bristly legs
Setae on a greenbottle's legs are sensitive to touch and air movements. They can also become coated with germs.

Soak food
The fly moistens the food with saliva and digestive juices containing enzymes.

Make soup
The enzymes break down the food, turning it into a liquid soup. The food is partially digested.

Eat food
Once the food has been liquified, it is soaked up by the fly's spongelike mouthparts. It is then sucked up the proboscis.

Greenbottle's proboscis

Housefly tongue
Tubes in pads at the end of the proboscis channel saliva down and liquid food up.

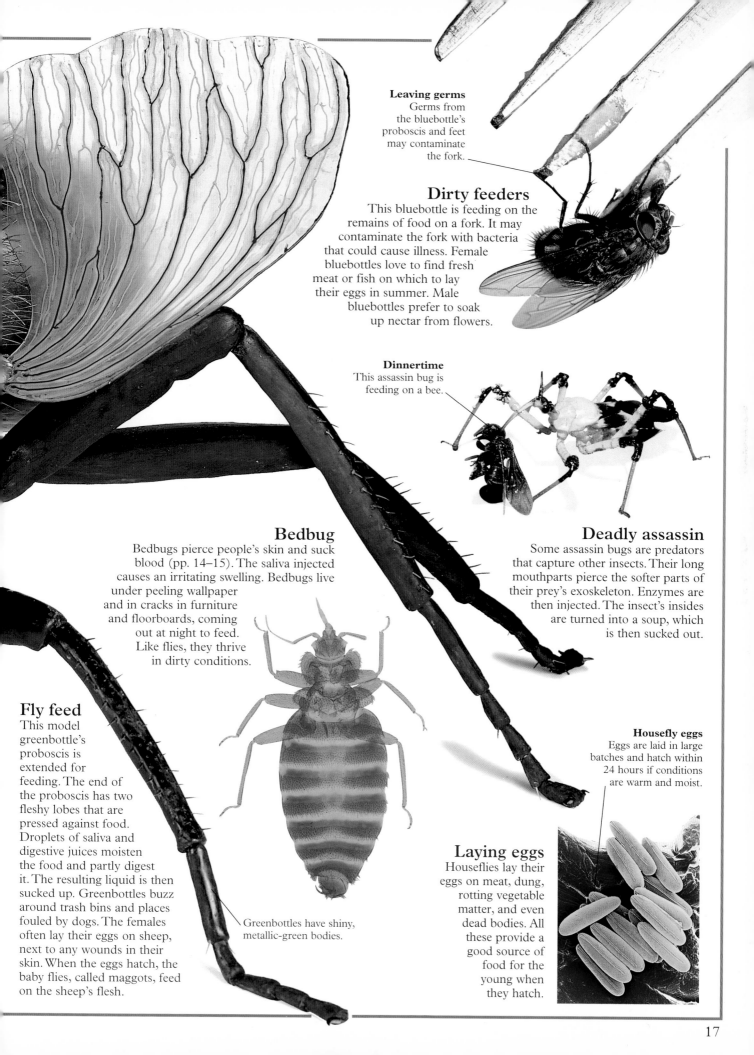

Leaving germs
Germs from the bluebottle's proboscis and feet may contaminate the fork.

Dirty feeders
This bluebottle is feeding on the remains of food on a fork. It may contaminate the fork with bacteria that could cause illness. Female bluebottles love to find fresh meat or fish on which to lay their eggs in summer. Male bluebottles prefer to soak up nectar from flowers.

Dinnertime
This assassin bug is feeding on a bee.

Bedbug
Bedbugs pierce people's skin and suck blood (pp. 14–15). The saliva injected causes an irritating swelling. Bedbugs live under peeling wallpaper and in cracks in furniture and floorboards, coming out at night to feed. Like flies, they thrive in dirty conditions.

Deadly assassin
Some assassin bugs are predators that capture other insects. Their long mouthparts pierce the softer parts of their prey's exoskeleton. Enzymes are then injected. The insect's insides are turned into a soup, which is then sucked out.

Fly feed
This model greenbottle's proboscis is extended for feeding. The end of the proboscis has two fleshy lobes that are pressed against food. Droplets of saliva and digestive juices moisten the food and partly digest it. The resulting liquid is then sucked up. Greenbottles buzz around trash bins and places fouled by dogs. The females often lay their eggs on sheep, next to any wounds in their skin. When the eggs hatch, the baby flies, called maggots, feed on the sheep's flesh.

Greenbottles have shiny, metallic-green bodies.

Housefly eggs
Eggs are laid in large batches and hatch within 24 hours if conditions are warm and moist.

Laying eggs
Houseflies lay their eggs on meat, dung, rotting vegetable matter, and even dead bodies. All these provide a good source of food for the young when they hatch.

Breathing holes

Insects breathe by taking in air, containing oxygen, through a series of holes called spiracles. Spiracles are found along each side of the body. They can be opened and closed to control the passage of air in and out. The spiracles are connected to a series of branching tubes called tracheae. These divide into finer branches that take oxygen to all the tissues. Most of the waste gas from respiration, carbon dioxide, passes through the tracheae and out of the spiracles. Some carbon dioxide is also lost through the body surface. Active insects have air sacs connected to the tracheae. Body movements help squeeze air in and out of these sacs. In this way, enough oxygen reaches the hard-working muscles. When an insect molts its exoskeleton, it must also shed its tracheae because they are connected to the exoskeleton.

Flying locust

Caterpillar
The spiracles of the peacock moth caterpillar look like orange ovals when closed.

First spiracles
The air supply to the locust's head is drawn into the body through the first pair of spiracles.

Brain power
The tracheae in the head supply oxygen to the brain and sense organs.

Tracheae
This model of the inside of a locust shows its breathing system. A single breathing tube is called a trachea. Two or more are called tracheae. The tracheae are supported by a series of spiral ridges that give them both strength and flexibility so that when an insect curves its body or takes in masses of food, they can bend and stay open.

The gills
Oxygen passes from the water through the thin surface of the gills into the tracheae inside.

Tough wall
The tracheae are made of the same tough material, chitin, as the exoskeleton.

Second spiracles
The second spiracle can be seen here on the outside of the locust. This is where a trachea meets the exoskeleton.

Damselfly nymph
In its young stages a damselfly is called a nymph and lives in freshwater. It breathes through a set of three gills at the tip of its abdomen.

Wing buds
Long wing buds show this is a mature nymph.

Helpful holes
There is a single muscle inside the locust's second spiracle that keeps the spiracle closed. When the muscle relaxes, the "lips" spring apart and the spiracle opens. Other spiracles can have two sets of muscles, one for opening and the other for closing. Being able to close the spiracles helps prevent loss of body moisture. This is especially important for insects that live in dry places.

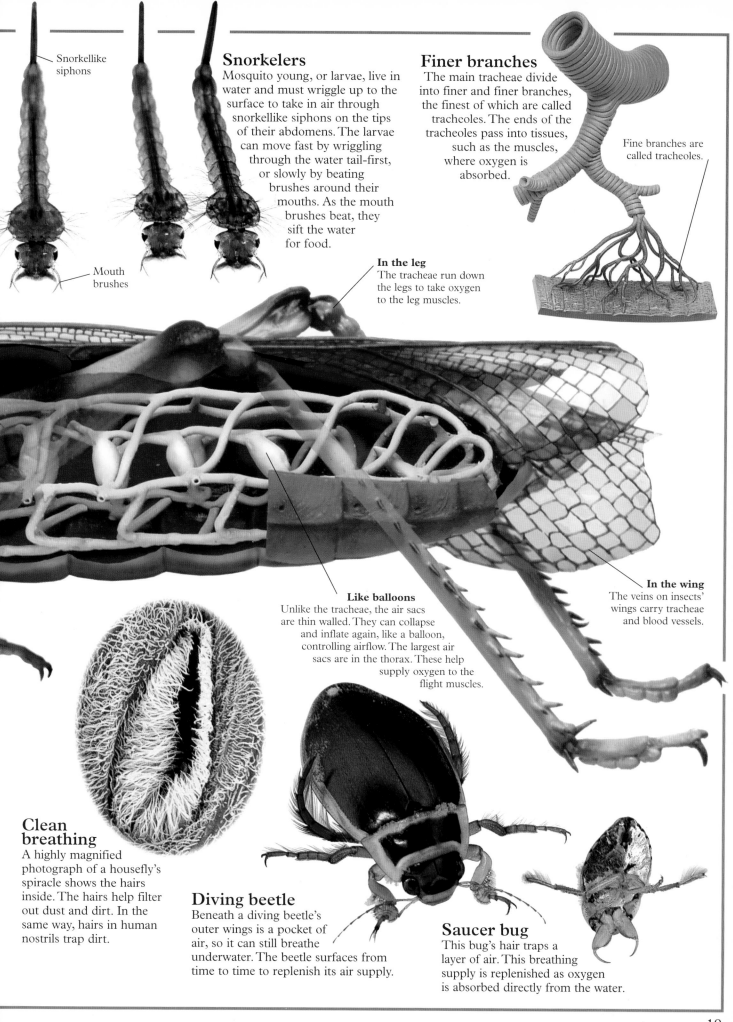

Snorkellike siphons

Snorkelers
Mosquito young, or larvae, live in water and must wriggle up to the surface to take in air through snorkellike siphons on the tips of their abdomens. The larvae can move fast by wriggling through the water tail-first, or slowly by beating brushes around their mouths. As the mouth brushes beat, they sift the water for food.

Mouth brushes

Finer branches
The main tracheae divide into finer and finer branches, the finest of which are called tracheoles. The ends of the tracheoles pass into tissues, such as the muscles, where oxygen is absorbed.

Fine branches are called tracheoles.

In the leg
The tracheae run down the legs to take oxygen to the leg muscles.

In the wing
The veins on insects' wings carry tracheae and blood vessels.

Like balloons
Unlike the tracheae, the air sacs are thin walled. They can collapse and inflate again, like a balloon, controlling airflow. The largest air sacs are in the thorax. These help supply oxygen to the flight muscles.

Clean breathing
A highly magnified photograph of a housefly's spiracle shows the hairs inside. The hairs help filter out dust and dirt. In the same way, hairs in human nostrils trap dirt.

Diving beetle
Beneath a diving beetle's outer wings is a pocket of air, so it can still breathe underwater. The beetle surfaces from time to time to replenish its air supply.

Saucer bug
This bug's hair traps a layer of air. This breathing supply is replenished as oxygen is absorbed directly from the water.

Bug-eyed

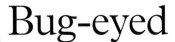

Insects' large, bulging eyes, like the eyes in this model of a horsefly's head, can seem creepy. They are very different from human eyes. Insects have compound eyes composed of many tiny eyelets (ommatidia). The more important sight is to an insect, the larger the eyes and the more eyelets it has. The female horsefly, for example, needs good eyesight to find the animals and people from whom she sucks blood. Each eyelet picks up only part of the field of vision. The individual signals are probably interpreted by the brain as a mosaic image. This type of eye is good at detecting movement because many eyelets are stimulated as something moves across the insect's vision.

Six-sided lens
Light enters each eyelet through these lenses.

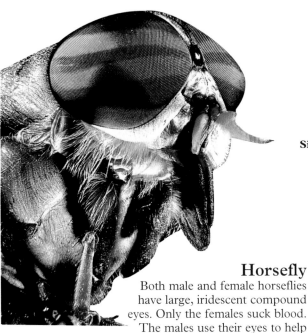

Horsefly
Both male and female horseflies have large, iridescent compound eyes. Only the females suck blood. The males use their eyes to help them find sugary substances on which to feed.

Stripes and bands
The brightly banded pattern on a horsefly's compound eye is due to light waves bouncing off the surface of the lenses. In doing so, some light waves are canceled out and others enhanced. This phenomenon is known as interference. Grasshoppers and dragonflies have stripes and spots on their eyes. This is due to different concentrations of pigments in the cells surrounding the cone-shaped lenses.

Eye protectors
A robberfly catches insect prey in midair. The hairs on its face help protect its eyes from the struggling victim.

All around vision
A dragonfly has large compound eyes that meet on top of its head. It can see above, below, sideways, and behind as it flies along.

Far apart
The widely spaced eyes of this damselfly help it judge distances. It can also rotate its head on its narrow neck.

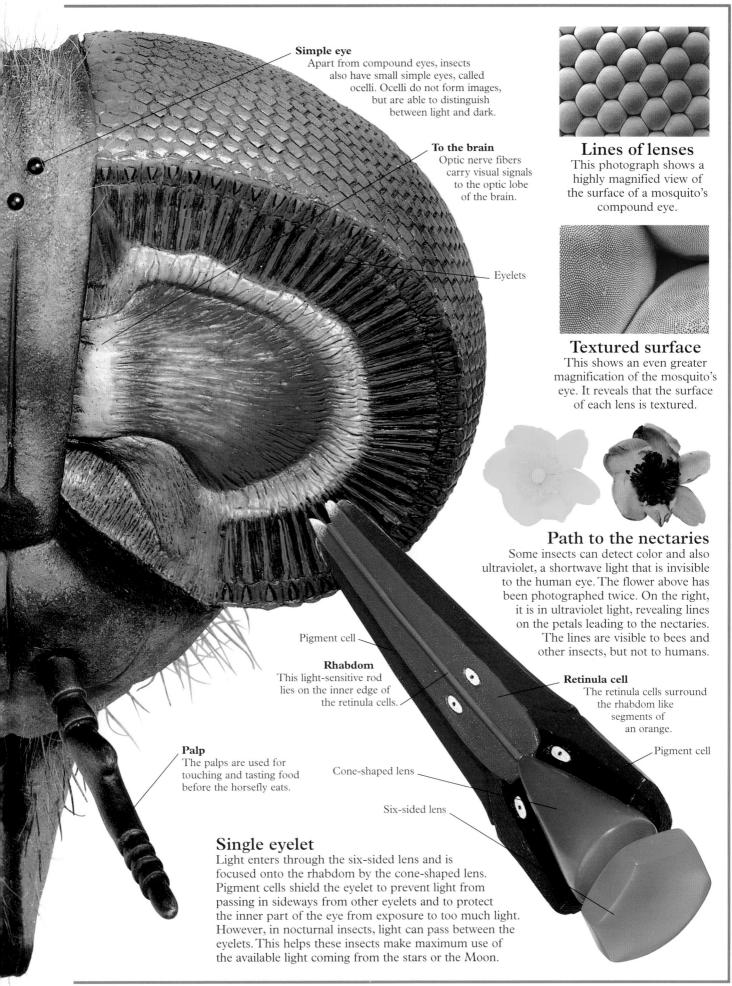

Simple eye
Apart from compound eyes, insects also have small simple eyes, called ocelli. Ocelli do not form images, but are able to distinguish between light and dark.

To the brain
Optic nerve fibers carry visual signals to the optic lobe of the brain.

Eyelets

Lines of lenses
This photograph shows a highly magnified view of the surface of a mosquito's compound eye.

Textured surface
This shows an even greater magnification of the mosquito's eye. It reveals that the surface of each lens is textured.

Path to the nectaries
Some insects can detect color and also ultraviolet, a shortwave light that is invisible to the human eye. The flower above has been photographed twice. On the right, it is in ultraviolet light, revealing lines on the petals leading to the nectaries. The lines are visible to bees and other insects, but not to humans.

Pigment cell

Rhabdom
This light-sensitive rod lies on the inner edge of the retinula cells.

Retinula cell
The retinula cells surround the rhabdom like segments of an orange.

Pigment cell

Palp
The palps are used for touching and tasting food before the horsefly eats.

Cone-shaped lens

Six-sided lens

Single eyelet
Light enters through the six-sided lens and is focused onto the rhabdom by the cone-shaped lens. Pigment cells shield the eyelet to prevent light from passing in sideways from other eyelets and to protect the inner part of the eye from exposure to too much light. However, in nocturnal insects, light can pass between the eyelets. This helps these insects make maximum use of the available light coming from the stars or the Moon.

Feeling the way

Insects' antennae are sometimes called feelers, but they can do a lot more than feel. Antennae carry a variety of different sense receptors. In some insects, such as male midges and mosquitoes, antennae are so sensitive to air movements and sound waves that they act as ears. A fly's antennae can assess flight speed by measuring the air flowing past. The antennae of some insects can pick up airborne odors. For example, a male emperor moth can smell a female several miles away by using his antennae. Antennae also carry taste receptors that are stimulated when they come into contact with food. Other parts of an insect's body have sense receptors, too. For example, the numerous hairs on the legs and bodies of insects are sensitive to touch.

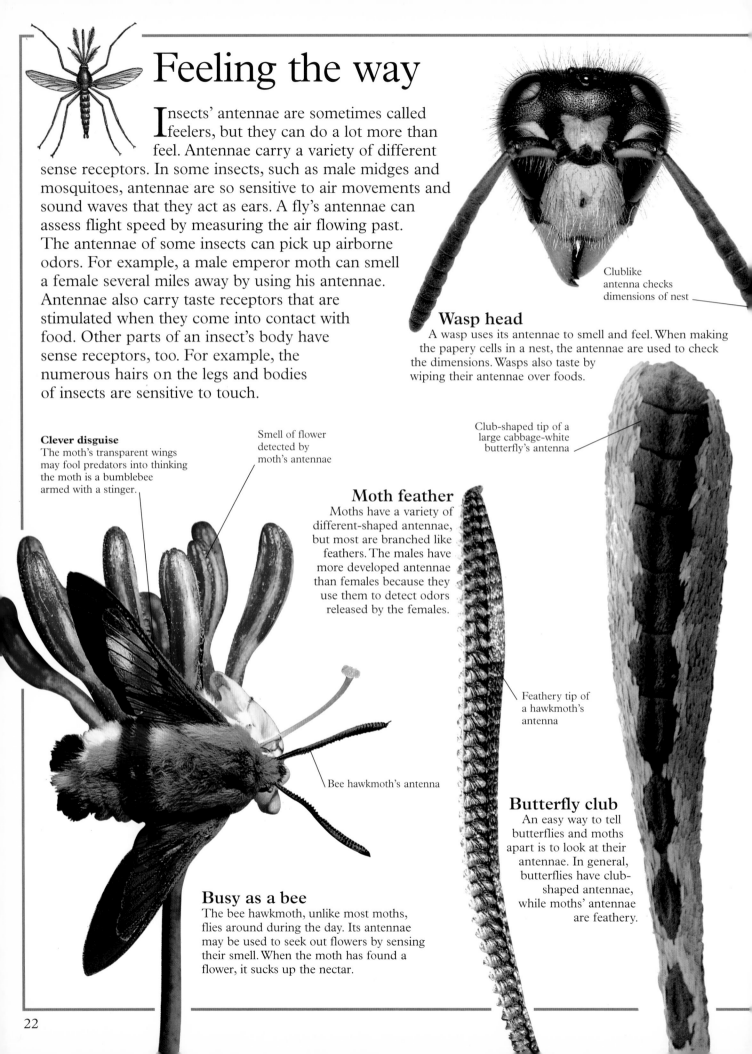

Clublike antenna checks dimensions of nest

Wasp head
A wasp uses its antennae to smell and feel. When making the papery cells in a nest, the antennae are used to check the dimensions. Wasps also taste by wiping their antennae over foods.

Clever disguise
The moth's transparent wings may fool predators into thinking the moth is a bumblebee armed with a stinger.

Smell of flower detected by moth's antennae

Club-shaped tip of a large cabbage-white butterfly's antenna

Moth feather
Moths have a variety of different-shaped antennae, but most are branched like feathers. The males have more developed antennae than females because they use them to detect odors released by the females.

Feathery tip of a hawkmoth's antenna

Bee hawkmoth's antenna

Busy as a bee
The bee hawkmoth, unlike most moths, flies around during the day. Its antennae may be used to seek out flowers by sensing their smell. When the moth has found a flower, it sucks up the nectar.

Butterfly club
An easy way to tell butterflies and moths apart is to look at their antennae. In general, butterflies have club-shaped antennae, while moths' antennae are feathery.

22

Cave dweller
This cricket was found in a cave in central Nigeria.

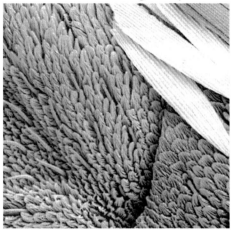

In the dark
The exceptionally long antennae of the cave cricket help it find its way inside dark caves. The antennae are sensitive to air currents and vibrations, and alert the cricket to other creatures moving nearby.

Nerve fibers to transmit signal

Pore chamber where odors collect

Body of nerve cell

Hair trigger
Certain setae (hairs) detect odors through a series of pores in their walls. The odors trigger nerve impulses. Male silkmoths have as many as 3,000 pores on each sensory hair on their antennae. There are 17,000 of these hairs on each antenna, all devoted to picking up odors produced by the female.

A closer look
With higher magnification under an electron microscope, the sensory hairs of the large cabbage-white butterfly's antenna can be seen close-up. Two types of sensory hairs are visible.

Bent antenna
The antennae of all weevils are bent like an elbow and project from the snout.

Sensory surface
By using an electron microscope, the sensory hairs and scales of a large cabbage-white butterfly's antenna are revealed. The hairs detect certain odors, such as the scent of the particular flowers that the butterfly visits to feed on. They also detect the odor of the particular leaves on which the female lays her eggs. If the antennae are removed, the butterfly can still smell using its other receptors.

Sensitive hairs
The sensory hairs on the tip of the antenna come into contact with the surface of a plant before a weevil feeds.

Bushy snouts
Male brush-snouted weevils use their bushy snouts to fence with other males when competing for females.

Plant probing
The brush-snouted weevil is a beetle with a long snout. It feeds on plants and the female lays her eggs in plant tissues, including freshly fallen tree trunks, seeds, and nuts. By probing the plant surface with the ends of its antennae, the weevil picks up chemical clues that help it detect good food.

Sound bugs

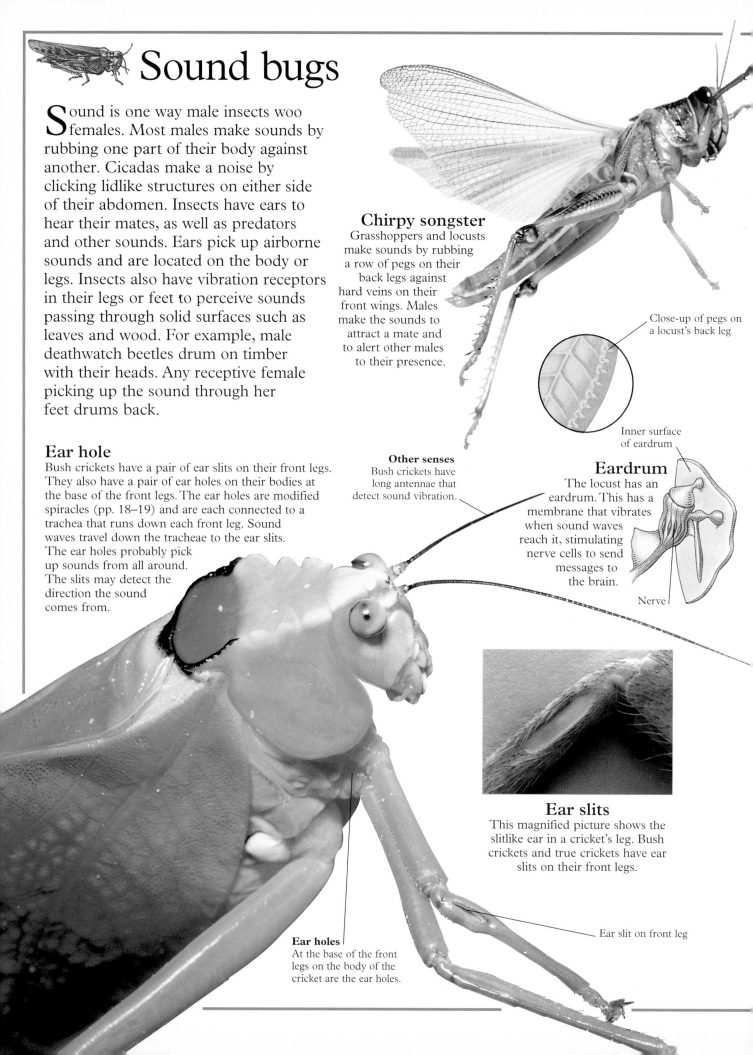

Sound is one way male insects woo females. Most males make sounds by rubbing one part of their body against another. Cicadas make a noise by clicking lidlike structures on either side of their abdomen. Insects have ears to hear their mates, as well as predators and other sounds. Ears pick up airborne sounds and are located on the body or legs. Insects also have vibration receptors in their legs or feet to perceive sounds passing through solid surfaces such as leaves and wood. For example, male deathwatch beetles drum on timber with their heads. Any receptive female picking up the sound through her feet drums back.

Chirpy songster

Grasshoppers and locusts make sounds by rubbing a row of pegs on their back legs against hard veins on their front wings. Males make the sounds to attract a mate and to alert other males to their presence.

Close-up of pegs on a locust's back leg

Inner surface of eardrum

Eardrum

The locust has an eardrum. This has a membrane that vibrates when sound waves reach it, stimulating nerve cells to send messages to the brain.

Nerve

Ear hole

Bush crickets have a pair of ear slits on their front legs. They also have a pair of ear holes on their bodies at the base of the front legs. The ear holes are modified spiracles (pp. 18–19) and are each connected to a trachea that runs down each front leg. Sound waves travel down the tracheae to the ear slits. The ear holes probably pick up sounds from all around. The slits may detect the direction the sound comes from.

Other senses

Bush crickets have long antennae that detect sound vibration.

Ear slits

This magnified picture shows the slitlike ear in a cricket's leg. Bush crickets and true crickets have ear slits on their front legs.

Ear slit on front leg

Ear holes

At the base of the front legs on the body of the cricket are the ear holes.

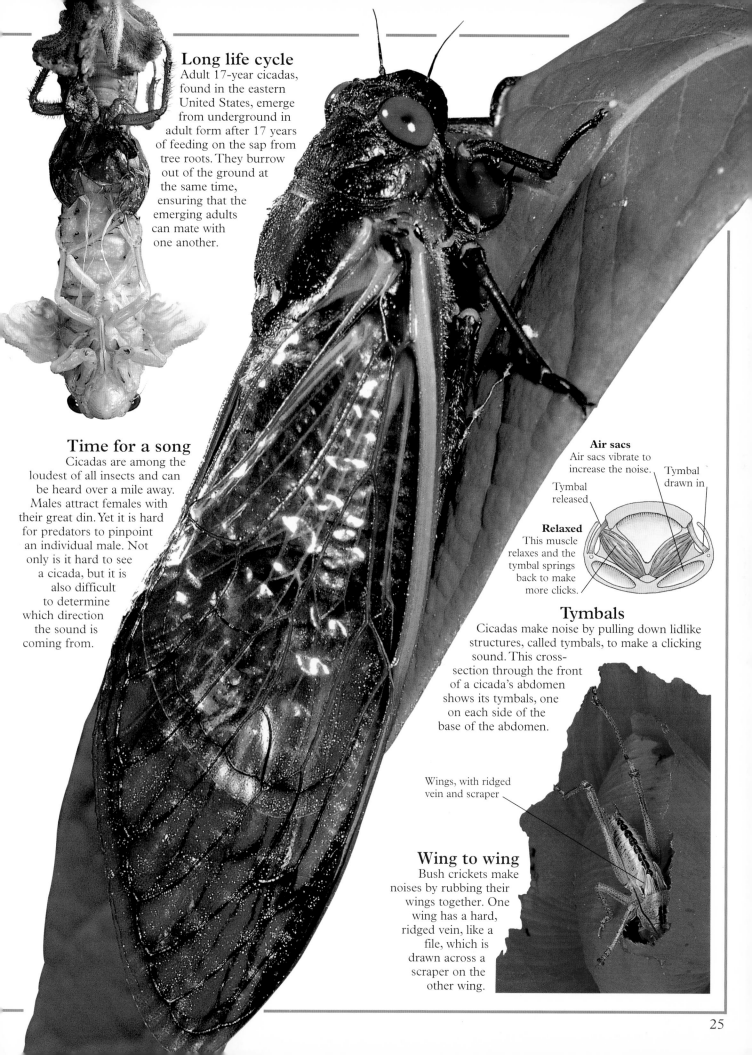

Long life cycle

Adult 17-year cicadas, found in the eastern United States, emerge from underground in adult form after 17 years of feeding on the sap from tree roots. They burrow out of the ground at the same time, ensuring that the emerging adults can mate with one another.

Time for a song

Cicadas are among the loudest of all insects and can be heard over a mile away. Males attract females with their great din. Yet it is hard for predators to pinpoint an individual male. Not only is it hard to see a cicada, but it is also difficult to determine which direction the sound is coming from.

Air sacs
Air sacs vibrate to increase the noise.

Tymbal drawn in

Tymbal released

Relaxed
This muscle relaxes and the tymbal springs back to make more clicks.

Tymbals

Cicadas make noise by pulling down lidlike structures, called tymbals, to make a clicking sound. This cross-section through the front of a cicada's abdomen shows its tymbals, one on each side of the base of the abdomen.

Wings, with ridged vein and scraper

Wing to wing

Bush crickets make noises by rubbing their wings together. One wing has a hard, ridged vein, like a file, which is drawn across a scraper on the other wing.

Leg power

Inside an insect's slender legs are the muscles that make them bend. However, the muscles that provide the power for walking, running, or swimming are all in the thorax. When walking and running, three of an insect's six legs are usually in contact with the ground at any one time. These form a stable tripod, with the front and back legs on one side of the insect's body, and the middle leg on the other side, touching the ground. Insects can use their front legs for a number of different tasks. Praying mantises use their front legs for catching prey.

Many beetles have heavy body armor, but they can still walk, run, and fly.

Lining up
The praying mantis hunts other insects, such as this fly. By swaying from side to side, each of its eyes gets a clear view of the prey.

Juicy fly, still unaware of the mantis's presence

Folding leg
When at rest, the thin tip of the leg folds back. The mantis places this part of the leg on the ground when it walks.

Legs away
The mantis moves slowly forward and begins to unfold its front legs. The fly can take off in a split second, so the mantis has to be careful not to be seen until the fly is within reach.

Death trap
The fly is trapped between the sharp spikes on the mantis's front legs so there is no chance it can escape. To be extra sure, mantises sometimes bite off their prey's wings and legs and discard them before feasting on the body.

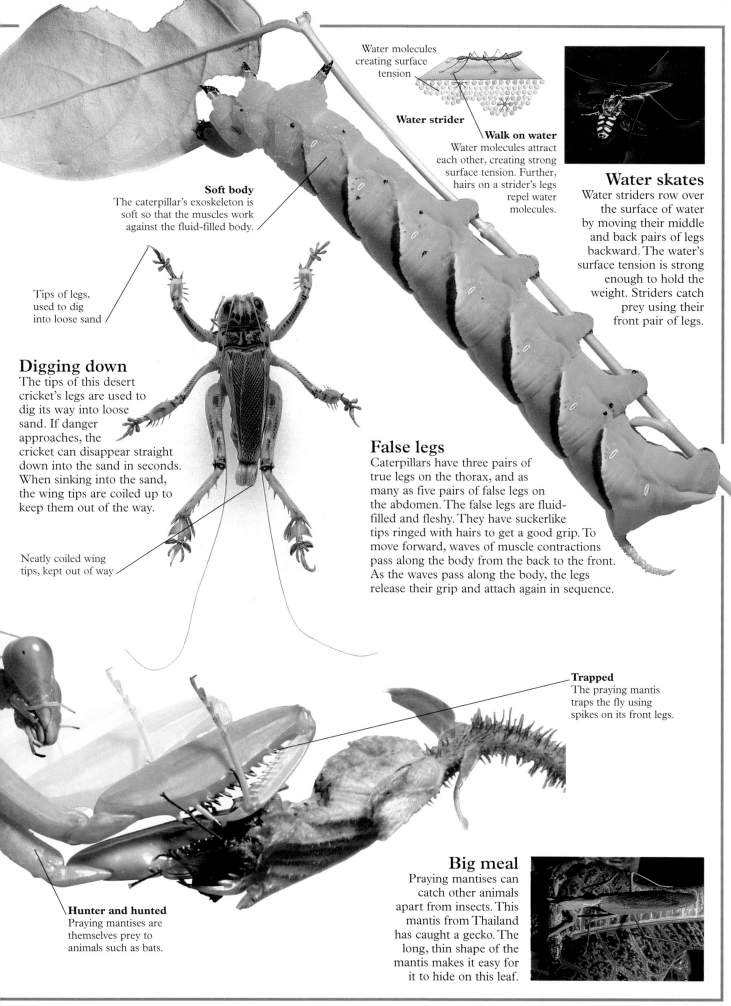

Water molecules creating surface tension

Water strider

Walk on water
Water molecules attract each other, creating strong surface tension. Further, hairs on a strider's legs repel water molecules.

Water skates
Water striders row over the surface of water by moving their middle and back pairs of legs backward. The water's surface tension is strong enough to hold the weight. Striders catch prey using their front pair of legs.

Soft body
The caterpillar's exoskeleton is soft so that the muscles work against the fluid-filled body.

Tips of legs, used to dig into loose sand

Digging down
The tips of this desert cricket's legs are used to dig its way into loose sand. If danger approaches, the cricket can disappear straight down into the sand in seconds. When sinking into the sand, the wing tips are coiled up to keep them out of the way.

Neatly coiled wing tips, kept out of way

False legs
Caterpillars have three pairs of true legs on the thorax, and as many as five pairs of false legs on the abdomen. The false legs are fluid-filled and fleshy. They have suckerlike tips ringed with hairs to get a good grip. To move forward, waves of muscle contractions pass along the body from the back to the front. As the waves pass along the body, the legs release their grip and attach again in sequence.

Trapped
The praying mantis traps the fly using spikes on its front legs.

Hunter and hunted
Praying mantises are themselves prey to animals such as bats.

Big meal
Praying mantises can catch other animals apart from insects. This mantis from Thailand has caught a gecko. The long, thin shape of the mantis makes it easy for it to hide on this leaf.

High jump

When it comes to jumping, fleas are among the champions of their body size. These models show a cat flea jumping. A cat flea can leap 13.39 in (34 cm) high – at least one hundred times its own body length! Fleas keep jumping until they find an animal from which to suck blood. They are able to jump hundreds of times an hour for several days. The key to this extraordinary feat is two pads of a rubbery material called resilin. These pads sit at the base of the flea's back legs. They are the remains of wing hinges, passed on from the flea's winged ancestors. Resilin stores and releases energy.

Sand flea
This may have got its name because it jumps like a flea. However, it is not an insect. It is a crustacean, like a crab.

Springtail
Springtails are tiny insects that live in soil. They escape danger by flicking down their forked tails. When the tail hits the ground, the springtail is propelled into the air. At other times, the tail is held against the lower part of the body.

Back leg section

Catch engaged

Resilin pad depressed

Coxa

Click beetle
If you hold a click beetle upside down in your hand, it will bounce into the air with a click sound. The click mechanism consists of a peg and slot underneath the thorax. By curving the body, the peg is suddenly forced into the slot and the beetle is thrown upward.

Preparing to jump
Energy is stored in the resilin pad by contractions of muscles in the thorax and the coxa, the first leg segment. When the leg is in this position, a catch on the edge of the body plates is engaged.

Femur

Trochanter

At an angle
Fleas usually take off at an angle, but can also jump almost vertically into the air.

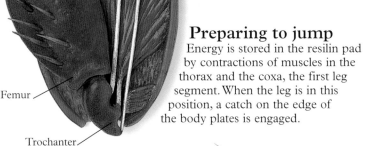

1 As a flea gets ready to jump, it bends its back legs. The femur, third leg segment, is nearly vertical. Next, the catch on the edge of the body plates is engaged. This prevents the release of energy stored in the resilin pad.

Coxa

Femur

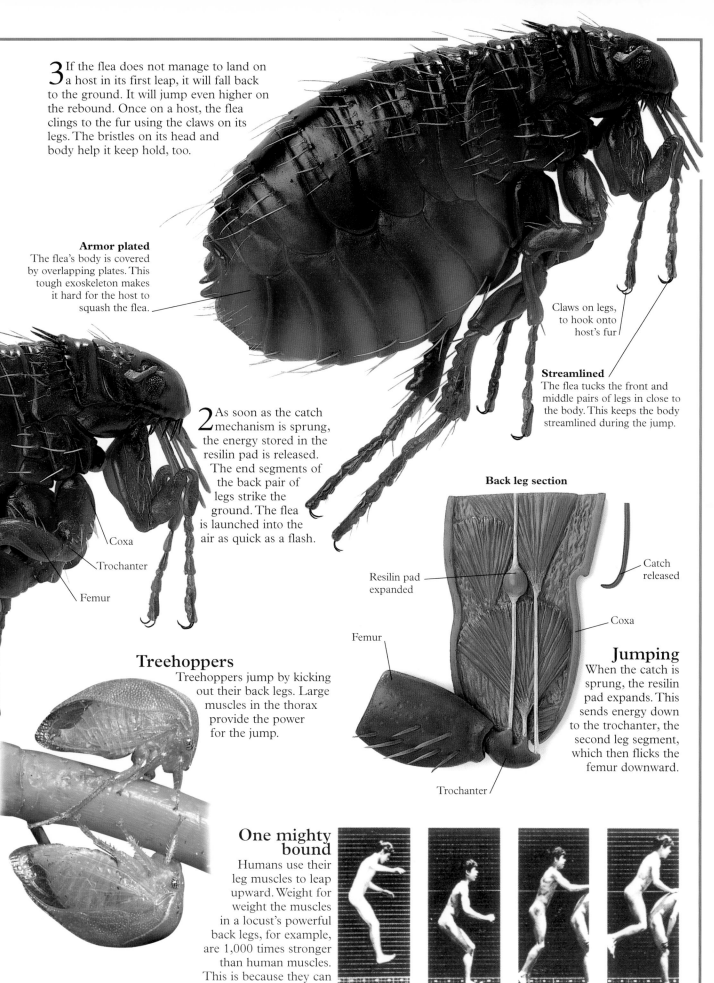

3 If the flea does not manage to land on a host in its first leap, it will fall back to the ground. It will jump even higher on the rebound. Once on a host, the flea clings to the fur using the claws on its legs. The bristles on its head and body help it keep hold, too.

Armor plated
The flea's body is covered by overlapping plates. This tough exoskeleton makes it hard for the host to squash the flea.

Claws on legs, to hook onto host's fur

Streamlined
The flea tucks the front and middle pairs of legs in close to the body. This keeps the body streamlined during the jump.

2 As soon as the catch mechanism is sprung, the energy stored in the resilin pad is released. The end segments of the back pair of legs strike the ground. The flea is launched into the air as quick as a flash.

Coxa

Trochanter

Femur

Back leg section

Resilin pad expanded

Catch released

Coxa

Femur

Jumping
When the catch is sprung, the resilin pad expands. This sends energy down to the trochanter, the second leg segment, which then flicks the femur downward.

Trochanter

Treehoppers
Treehoppers jump by kicking out their back legs. Large muscles in the thorax provide the power for the jump.

One mighty bound
Humans use their leg muscles to leap upward. Weight for weight the muscles in a locust's powerful back legs, for example, are 1,000 times stronger than human muscles. This is because they can contract more rapidly.

Taking flight

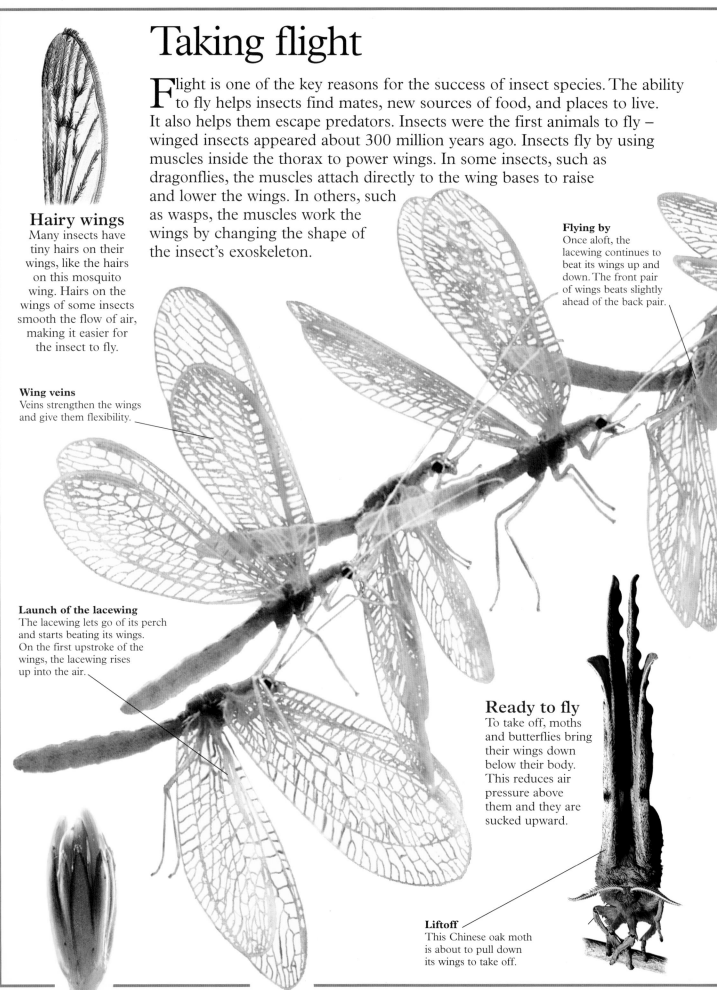

Flight is one of the key reasons for the success of insect species. The ability to fly helps insects find mates, new sources of food, and places to live. It also helps them escape predators. Insects were the first animals to fly – winged insects appeared about 300 million years ago. Insects fly by using muscles inside the thorax to power wings. In some insects, such as dragonflies, the muscles attach directly to the wing bases to raise and lower the wings. In others, such as wasps, the muscles work the wings by changing the shape of the insect's exoskeleton.

Hairy wings
Many insects have tiny hairs on their wings, like the hairs on this mosquito wing. Hairs on the wings of some insects smooth the flow of air, making it easier for the insect to fly.

Wing veins
Veins strengthen the wings and give them flexibility.

Flying by
Once aloft, the lacewing continues to beat its wings up and down. The front pair of wings beats slightly ahead of the back pair.

Launch of the lacewing
The lacewing lets go of its perch and starts beating its wings. On the first upstroke of the wings, the lacewing rises up into the air.

Ready to fly
To take off, moths and butterflies bring their wings down below their body. This reduces air pressure above them and they are sucked upward.

Liftoff
This Chinese oak moth is about to pull down its wings to take off.

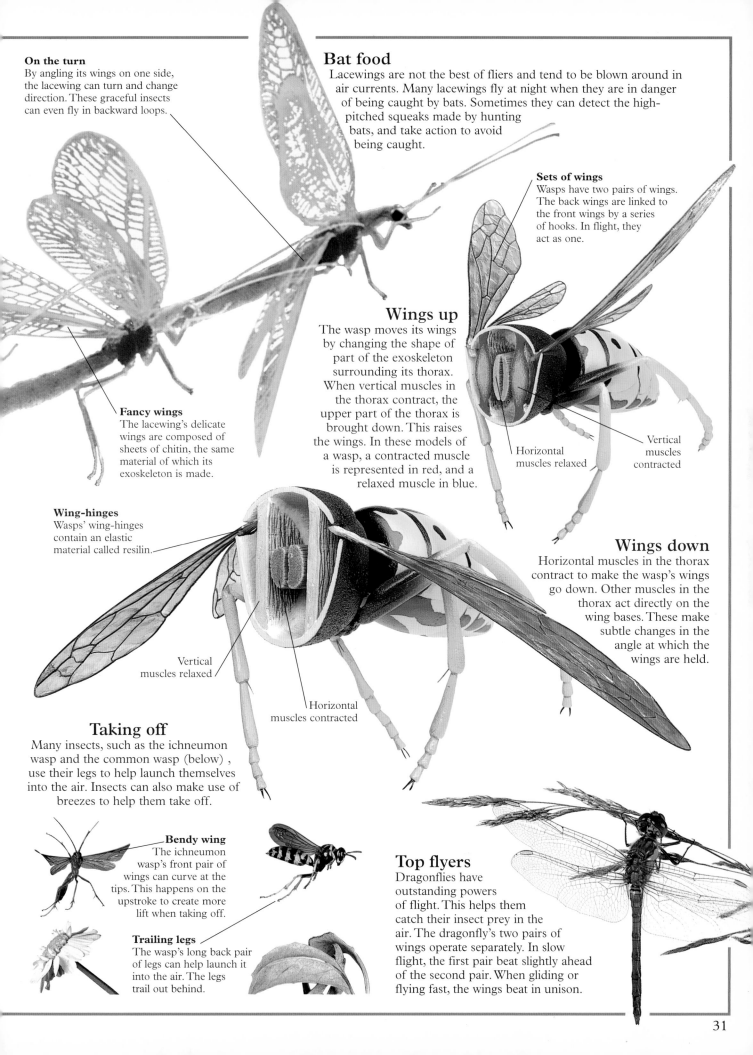

On the turn
By angling its wings on one side, the lacewing can turn and change direction. These graceful insects can even fly in backward loops.

Bat food
Lacewings are not the best of fliers and tend to be blown around in air currents. Many lacewings fly at night when they are in danger of being caught by bats. Sometimes they can detect the high-pitched squeaks made by hunting bats, and take action to avoid being caught.

Sets of wings
Wasps have two pairs of wings. The back wings are linked to the front wings by a series of hooks. In flight, they act as one.

Wings up
The wasp moves its wings by changing the shape of part of the exoskeleton surrounding its thorax. When vertical muscles in the thorax contract, the upper part of the thorax is brought down. This raises the wings. In these models of a wasp, a contracted muscle is represented in red, and a relaxed muscle in blue.

Horizontal muscles relaxed

Vertical muscles contracted

Fancy wings
The lacewing's delicate wings are composed of sheets of chitin, the same material of which its exoskeleton is made.

Wing-hinges
Wasps' wing-hinges contain an elastic material called resilin.

Vertical muscles relaxed

Horizontal muscles contracted

Wings down
Horizontal muscles in the thorax contract to make the wasp's wings go down. Other muscles in the thorax act directly on the wing bases. These make subtle changes in the angle at which the wings are held.

Taking off
Many insects, such as the ichneumon wasp and the common wasp (below) , use their legs to help launch themselves into the air. Insects can also make use of breezes to help them take off.

Bendy wing
The ichneumon wasp's front pair of wings can curve at the tips. This happens on the upstroke to create more lift when taking off.

Trailing legs
The wasp's long back pair of legs can help launch it into the air. The legs trail out behind.

Top flyers
Dragonflies have outstanding powers of flight. This helps them catch their insect prey in the air. The dragonfly's two pairs of wings operate separately. In slow flight, the first pair beat slightly ahead of the second pair. When gliding or flying fast, the wings beat in unison.

Unwelcome guests

Flying roach
Cockroaches that live in kitchens are not good fliers, like this monster. Instead they scuttle about, slipping under counters and behind cupboards with ease.

Largest flying cockroach

Cuckoos lay their eggs in other birds' nests. These birds care for the chicks when they hatch.

N
o one likes to think of insects living on them, but for the human head louse, a scalp makes an ideal home. Head lice need the warmth and shelter given by our hair, and blood sucked from our scalps makes the perfect meal. In fact, they cannot survive if removed from the head. A heavy infestation of head lice can cause extreme itching. Other insects can harm people and other animals by feeding inside them, just as plants can suffer from insects devouring the insides of their leaves, seeds, and other tissues. And there are also plenty of creatures that are simply annoying, from the kitchen cockroach to the deceiving cuckoo.

Holes in lid of egg to let in air

Louse nymph
A young head louse, called a nymph, is a smaller version of the adult.

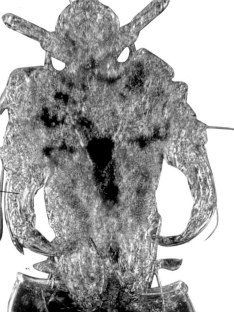

1 The eggs of head lice are called nits. A female head louse lays up to 100 eggs in her lifetime. Each one is only 0.039 in (1 mm) long and is cemented to a strand of hair.

2 The head louse nymph forces off the lid of its egg by swallowing air to make its body become larger. Fluid also collects in the front of the body, making it bulge outward.

New skin
The developing nymph's exoskeleton is shed along with the eggshell.

Nit closely attached to hair

Thick wall
A tough eggshell protects the developing nymph.

Egg laying
The long egg-laying tube is inside a protective sheath tipped with sense organs.

Parasitic wasp
Many kinds of small wasps lay their eggs in, or on, the young of other insects. When the eggs hatch, they feed on these young. Here, a wasp probes the surface of a log with her egg-laying tube to find an insect that is hiding inside.

Caterpillar dinner
Here, a wasp's young are coming out of a cabbage white butterfly's caterpillar after feeding on its insides.

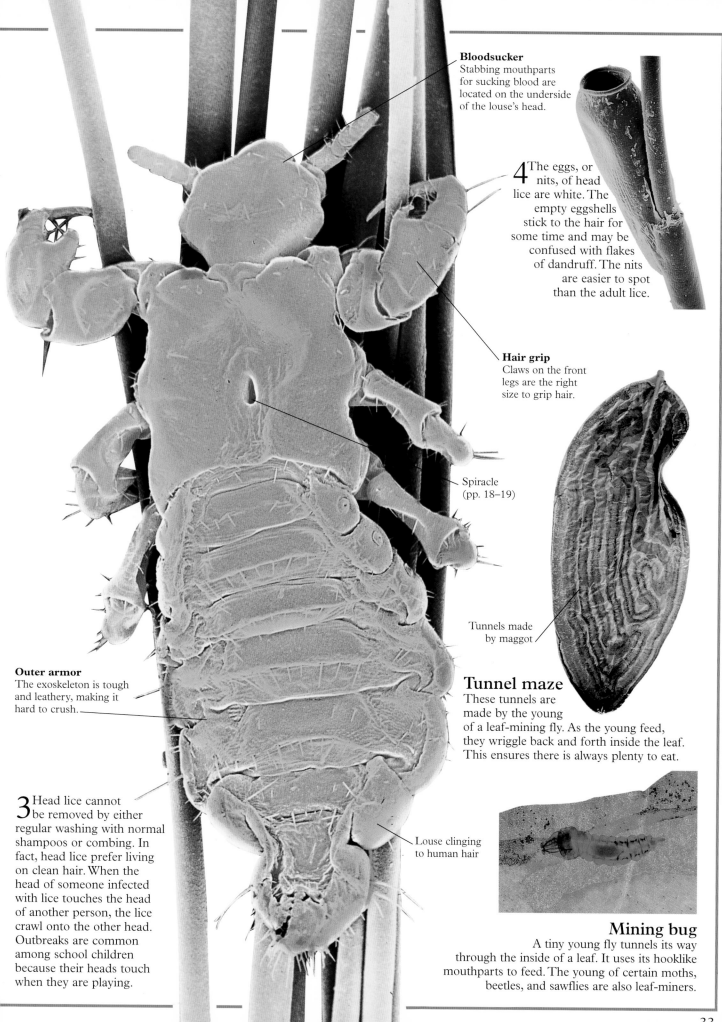

Bloodsucker
Stabbing mouthparts
for sucking blood are
located on the underside
of the louse's head.

4 The eggs, or
nits, of head
lice are white. The
empty eggshells
stick to the hair for
some time and may be
confused with flakes
of dandruff. The nits
are easier to spot
than the adult lice.

Hair grip
Claws on the front
legs are the right
size to grip hair.

Spiracle
(pp. 18–19)

Outer armor
The exoskeleton is tough
and leathery, making it
hard to crush.

Tunnels made
by maggot

Tunnel maze
These tunnels are
made by the young
of a leaf-mining fly. As the young feed,
they wriggle back and forth inside the leaf.
This ensures there is always plenty to eat.

3 Head lice cannot
be removed by either
regular washing with normal
shampoos or combing. In
fact, head lice prefer living
on clean hair. When the
head of someone infected
with lice touches the head
of another person, the lice
crawl onto the other head.
Outbreaks are common
among school children
because their heads touch
when they are playing.

Louse clinging
to human hair

Mining bug
A tiny young fly tunnels its way
through the inside of a leaf. It uses its hooklike
mouthparts to feed. The young of certain moths,
beetles, and sawflies are also leaf-miners.

33

Nectar collector

Ⓞne of the worker honeybee's many jobs is to collect nectar and pollen from flowers to feed the hive. The model below shows a worker honeybee at a broom flower. The bee's long tongue unfolds to lap up nectar, which the bee then stores in its crop. As the bee probes the flower, pollen collects on its head, hairy body, and legs. It will inadvertently pollinate another flower by transferring some of this pollen to the next flower of the same kind it visits. Back at the hive, the remaining pollen is mixed with honey and packed into wax cells. The nectar is passed from the bee's crop so it can be stored in the wax cells.

Queen and worker bees

Petal eater
The earwig goes from one flower to the next, eating petals. Pollen becomes attached to its body and is passed on to each flower, helping pollination.

Well groomed
Each antenna is kept clean by passing it through a notch on the front leg.

Uncoiled
Butterflies are also important pollinators of flowers. They suck up nectar through a long, tubelike tongue called a proboscis. The proboscis is coiled up when not in use.

Long tongue for sucking up nectar

Salivary glands
These glands in the head, and a pair in the thorax, produce saliva, which helps dissolve nectar.

Short mouthparts for sucking up blood

Spring blooms
As soon as the cold winter is over, bees come out to forage for food. They find nectar in the flowers that bloom early in the year, such as this crocus. They need to build up the hive's food reserves, which get depleted over the winter.

Long tongue
This horsefly from Nepal has dual-purpose mouthparts. It feeds on both blood and nectar.

Furry bee
A bumblebee has a lot of hair to keep it warm in the cool climates where it lives. It stores nectar and pollen in underground nests.

Worker head
A bee's tongue (glossa) is supported by other mouthparts when lapping up nectar. The mandibles have many uses. These include chewing pollen, molding wax and plant resins, grooming, and fighting.

Salivary glands

Mandible

Mouthparts to support the hairy tongue

Antenna

Glossa

The crop
The crop expands to take in, at the most, 0.0014 oz (40 mg) of nectar. This is equivalent in volume to a pinprick of blood.

The valve
A valve inside the gut stops nectar from passing from the crop into the midgut.

Rectum

Barbed sting

Hairy face
Pollen grains sit wedged among the hairs on a worker honeybee's face.

Pollen baskets
Most pollen is collected on rows of hairs called combs on the insides of the back legs. It is transferred to pollen baskets on the outsides of the back legs.

Pollen combs
Pollen on combs on the left back leg is transferred to the basket on the right back leg.

Busy bees
When a bee returns to its hive, it regurgitates the nectar it has collected and passes it with its glossa to the other workers. They place the nectar into wax cells where it matures into honey.

Getting together

Mating results in procreation and continues a species. Some insects attract their mates by producing scents, singing, or offering gifts of food. For others, looks are important, such as wing color in certain butterflies. Once a male and female are close together, touch can bring about mating. Many insects gather together in a swarm to mate, or meet where the female will lay her eggs. The males of most insects place sperm, or a package of sperm, directly inside the female. A few kinds of insects, such as springtails, put sperm packages on the ground, which the female picks up. Insect eggs are either fertilized by the sperm immediately, or the female can store the sperm for later use. A few insects, such as aphids, produce young without having to mate at all.

Many partners
Ladybugs may mate with several different partners, especially when there are many adults around.

Courting
Milkweed bugs often stroke each other's antennae before they mate.

Like a tortoise
A shieldlike thorax and wing cases give the tortoise beetle its name.

Small males
Male insects are often smaller than females, as in this pair of tortoise beetles, but the male beetle usually has to climb on top of the female to mate.

Great attraction
Male butterflies are often attracted by a female's wing size and colors. The females are attracted by scents produced by the males. Some male scents encourage the female to land, so mating can take place.

Ovaries
Eggs are produced in the ovaries inside the female. They pass down a channel to the egg-laying chamber, during which time they are fertilized by the stored sperm.

Mating
When milkweed bugs mate, the male climbs on top of the female, both facing the same way. He begins to insert his sperm-transmitting organ, called the aedeagus, into her body. Then he climbs down and turns around, so they face opposite directions. They stay in this position, as shown right, for up to five hours, until sperm has reached a storage space inside her body. After they separate, both may go on to mate with others.

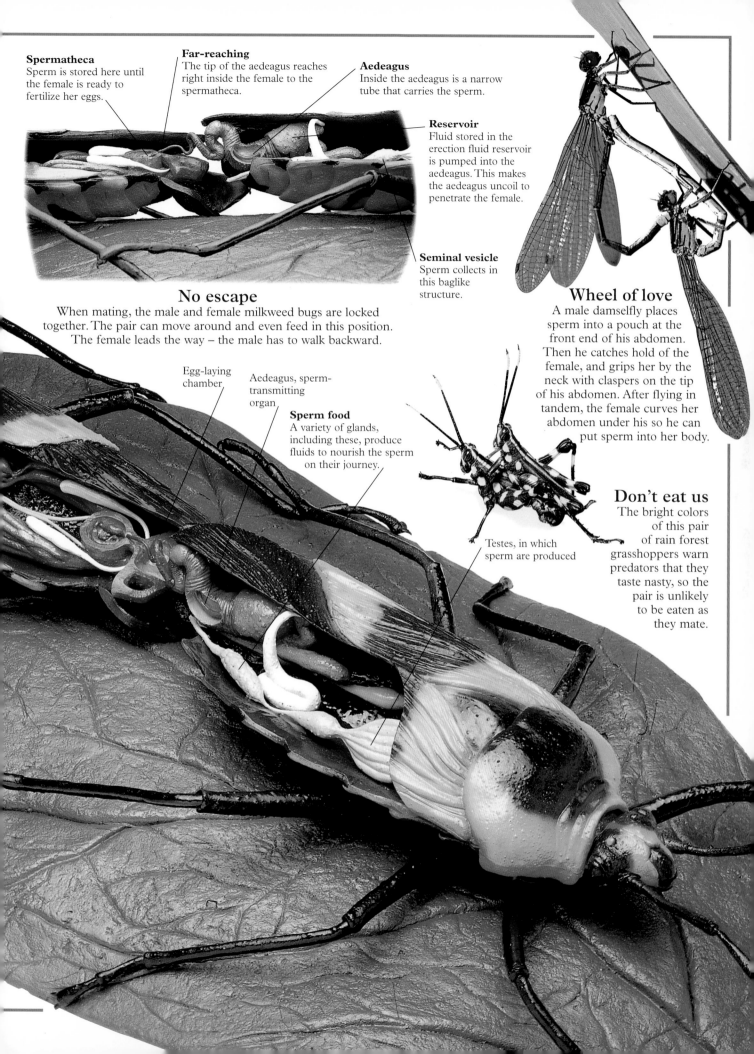

Spermatheca
Sperm is stored here until the female is ready to fertilize her eggs.

Far-reaching
The tip of the aedeagus reaches right inside the female to the spermatheca.

Aedeagus
Inside the aedeagus is a narrow tube that carries the sperm.

Reservoir
Fluid stored in the erection fluid reservoir is pumped into the aedeagus. This makes the aedeagus uncoil to penetrate the female.

Seminal vesicle
Sperm collects in this baglike structure.

No escape
When mating, the male and female milkweed bugs are locked together. The pair can move around and even feed in this position. The female leads the way – the male has to walk backward.

Egg-laying chamber

Aedeagus, sperm-transmitting organ

Sperm food
A variety of glands, including these, produce fluids to nourish the sperm on their journey.

Testes, in which sperm are produced

Wheel of love
A male damselfly places sperm into a pouch at the front end of his abdomen. Then he catches hold of the female, and grips her by the neck with claspers on the tip of his abdomen. After flying in tandem, the female curves her abdomen under his so he can put sperm into her body.

Don't eat us
The bright colors of this pair of rain forest grasshoppers warn predators that they taste nasty, so the pair is unlikely to be eaten as they mate.

New life

Insects are very careful where they lay their eggs. Many lay eggs on or near food, so when the young hatch, they have plenty to eat. The eggs are also laid in places where they are unlikely to be found and eaten themselves. They can be hidden under leaves or bark, or inside fruits or nuts. The eggs get some protection from their own shells, too, which also help keep in moisture. Some insects, such as cockroaches and praying mantises, will even pack their eggs into a special tough case. But truly attentive insect parents stay with their eggs and young to defend them from attackers. A few kinds of insects, such as aphids, do not lay eggs at all, giving birth to live young instead.

Head emerging from hole made by mandibles

Mother care

A female stinkbug guards her precious batch of eggs from enemies who would find them a tasty snack. Stinkbugs often use their bodies as shields to protect their eggs from certain kinds of tiny wasps. These wasps try to lay an egg of their own inside the stinkbug's eggs. When the wasp young hatches, it feeds on the bug's eggs and destroys them.

On guard
This stinkbug is using its body to protect its eggs.

Bursting eggs

Insect eggshells are tough, which makes it difficult for young to hatch. Caterpillars, like this tobacco budworm caterpillar, use their mandibles (pp. 14–15) to chew an escape hole out of their shell. The young of some other insects pop out through a special lid in their egg, or split it open along lines of weakness. Some young insects have special spines or teeth to help split the shell.

Foul smelling
Stinkbugs also keep away enemies by producing a foul-smelling substance from glands on the thorax between the middle and back legs.

Eggshell
The eggs get some protection from their own shells. When the stinkbug young hatch from the eggs, they will have exoskeletons to protect them.

Egg rows
The stinkbug's eggs are laid in tight rows around a plant stem.

Parent bug

Adult parent bug

After careful guarding, the eggs of the parent bug hatch into nymphs, young that look like miniature versions of their parents. The only things they lack are functional wings. Many members of the true bug family (pp. 8–9) guard their eggs and young. In most cases, it is the female that protects them, but males of some species do take on the job. Some males have no choice: females glue the eggs to their backs, so they have to watch over them until they hatch.

Young parent bug

Ready meals

The eggs of fruit flies are often laid in rotting fruit, which the young feed on when they hatch. A single female can lay several thousands of eggs.

Acorn shelter

When ready to lay an egg, a female acorn weevil finds a newly formed acorn on an oak tree. She drills a hole in the acorn using the tiny set of jaws at the end of her long snout. As she drills deeper and deeper, the weevil feeds on the acorn's tissues. When she has finished drilling, she withdraws her snout, turns around, places her ovipositor (egg-laying tube) in the hole, and lays an egg. Deep within the acorn, the egg hatches, and the young begins to feed on the acorn. It is an ideal nursery, providing both food and shelter. When the acorn falls from the oak tree, the young weevil crawls out. It then burrows into the soil where it turns into a pupa, ready to become an adult weevil.

Colored egg
The egg in this magnified photograph has been dyed blue for clarity.

Life changes

The young of some insects look like miniature versions of their parents. These young are usually called nymphs. When nymphs first hatch, they lack wings. Then they go through a series of molts, acquiring wing pads before becoming fully winged adults. Other insects go through more drastic changes in their lives. They hatch out as young, such as caterpillars, maggots, and grubs, that are all called larvae. Larvae also go through a series of molts, growing bigger with each one. A fully grown larva turns into a pupa, and from that an adult emerges. But whether an insect starts life as a nymph or larva, it cannot grow as an adult. Unlike their young, insects cannot shed their exoskeletons.

Pad of silk spun by caterpillar

Bird dropping
This comma butterfly caterpillar has a white streak running down its back. This makes it look like a bird dropping, protecting it from predators.

1 When a caterpillar is fully grown, it finds a twig or stem from which to hang, usually in dense vegetation. Wherever it settles, the caterpillar spins a pad of silk, attaching itself to its support.

Chrysalis hanging from silken pads by hooks

2 The caterpillar sheds its soft exoskeleton for the last time to reveal its pupal stage, called a chrysalis. The chrysalis hangs onto the silken pad by hooks at its tip.

3 The surface of the chrysalis hardens to protect the adult developing inside. The chrysalis looks like a dead leaf, and so does not attract the attention of predators. The chrysalis stage lasts about 15 days.

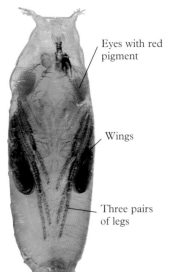

Eyes with red pigment

Wings

Three pairs of legs

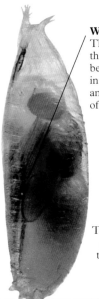

Wing width
The width of the wings can be seen clearly in this side-angled view of the maggot.

Last stage
The transparent exoskeleton of the last maggot stage protects the pupa.

 Fruit fly maggot
This picture shows the actual size of a fruit fly maggot.

Becoming a fly
Magnified images of a fruit fly maggot show its insides developing. The exoskeleton of the last stage of the fruit fly's maggot protects its pupa. Within this pupa, the maggot's body is almost completely transformed into an adult fly. Soon the fly will split open its old exoskeleton and begin its adult life.

Changes within

The insides, as well as the outsides, of the caterpillar change with each new stage. All the stages have a tubular heart along the top and a nerve cord below. The reproductive organs (colored red) develop to become functional in the adult stage.

Caterpillar
Caterpillars have a simple tubelike gut to digest the quantities of greenery they eat.

Chrysalis
In the chrysalis, the body is rearranged into that of the adult. The gut becomes coiled to cope with liquid food.

Adult
The reproductive organs are fully developed.

4 When the chrysalis splits open, a butterfly pulls its body free. The butterfly's wings are soft and wrinkled.

5 To fully extend the wings, blood is pumped through the wing veins. The tubelike proboscis (pp. 16–17) is also extended using blood pressure. When the wings are dry, the butterfly will search for flowers from which to suck nectar. Depending on the time of year, it may seek a mate or simply find a tree trunk to rest on.

White comma
The white comma-shaped mark gives this butterfly its name. The mark's real purpose is camouflage – it resembles a hole in a leaf.

Balloon flight
The wing is like a bag that would expand into a balloon if it were not for tiny ligaments that hold the upper and lower membranes together.

Ragged wing
The ragged wing edges and brown outer surface help the butterfly blend in with dead leaves when resting.

41

Glossary

A

Abdomen An insect divides into three regions: the head, the thorax, and the abdomen. The abdomen is at the rear of the insect.

Antennae All insects have one pair of antennae attached to the head. Antennae are segmented. They are covered with tiny sensory structures called setae. Antennae are used in various different ways, including smelling, tasting, feeling, and hearing.

The mouthparts of a mosquito

C

Camouflage How an insect blends in with its surroundings. For example, some butterflies and moths have wings colored like leaves. Camouflage helps insects stay hidden from hungry predators. Furthermore, if the insect is a predator itself, such as a praying mantis, camouflage helps it remain unseen by its prey.

Chrysalis The name given to the pupa of a butterfly, inside of which the adult develops fully. The chrysalis is protected by a hard, shell-like coat.

Colony A social grouping of a large number of the same insects – ants for example – that build and live in a community, dividing work according to specific tasks for the benefit of all.

Compound eye Insect's eye that is composed of separate light-sensitive eyelets called ommatidia. The number of ommatidia ranges from a few to several thousand. Some insects have huge compound eyes that give them all-around vision.

Coxa
The first segment of an insect's leg that extends from the thorax.

D

Diaphragm Elastic membrane that supports and separates an insect's heart from the blood-filled space containing the other body organs, such as those in the digestive and reproductive systems.

Digestion The process whereby food is broken down by the action of enzymes in an insect's gut into waste products and the various nutrients necessary for life.

E

Enzyme A substance produced by cells in an insect's digestive system that helps in the chemical breakdown of food material.

Exoskeleton An insect's exoskeleton is an outer casing made up of layers containing chitin, a durable horny material. The exoskeleton supports and protects the insect's internal body organs. The insect's muscles are attached to the exoskeleton, as are parts of the internal organs. The tracheae are connected to the exoskeleton at the spiracles.

Bee pollinating a flower

F

Femur The third leg segment of an insect, joined to the trochanter.

G

Ganglia Nerve centers are made up of two ganglia. Running through an

Milkweed bugs mating on a leaf

A flea jumping

insect's body is a row of ganglia linked together by a nerve cord. The ganglia receive signals from and pass on signals to different parts of the body. The ganglia in the thorax can control the movement of an insect's legs and wings directly, operating independently of the brain.

H

Hindgut That part of an insect's digestive system located at the rear of the insect's abdomen, including the rectum and anus.

I

Insect An animal with a jointed exoskeleton, a body split into three parts (head, thorax, and abdomen), a pair of antennae, three pairs of legs, and one or two pairs of wings.

L

Larva One of the stages in the life cycle of an insect such as a caterpillar, grub, or maggot. The larva hatches from an egg, and its main function is to feed and grow. Larvae (plural of larva) have simple mouthparts, and can have legs. Larvae increase gradually in size before becoming pupae.

M

Malpighian tubules Attached to the point where the midgut and the hindgut meet, these structures remove waste products from an insect's blood. They work in a similar way to human kidneys. The waste products then pass into an insect's hindgut for removal from the body in its droppings.

Mandibles
These are an insect's jaws. In insects with chewing mouthparts, they are broad with a cutting edge. In insects with piercing and sucking mouthparts, the mandibles are narrow and pointed.

Horsefly's compound eye

N

Nectar
A thick, sugary substance, manufactured in the nectaries of flowers, upon which insects feed. As an insect feeds, the flower's pollen sticks to its body and legs. The pollen is then transported to other flowers of the same species that the insect visits, resulting in successful pollination.

Nymph
The term given to a young or immature insect whose life cycle does not involve a pupal stage. Nymphs hatch from eggs and gradually increase in size, developing wings and reproductive organs as they mature.

O

Ocelli
In addition to possessing compound eyes, insects have between one and three ocelli, or simple eyes. Ocelli can distinguish only varying amounts of light.

Ommatidia
The scientific name for the eyelets, or individual light-sensitive units, of an insect's compound eye. Each ommatidium has a six-sided lens at the surface and extends back to the nerve cells connected to the brain.

Ovipositor
A tubelike structure at the tip of a female insect's abdomen that deposits fertilized eggs in a safe place for their development.

P

Palp
One of a pair of sensory appendages belonging to an insect's mouthparts. Palps are used for touching and tasting food before an insect eats.

Parasite
Animal, plant, or insect that lives and feeds in or on another, usually doing some harm.

Pollination
Many insects transfer pollen, a fine, powdery substance, from one flower to another, so ensuring that seeds are produced.

Predator
An animal that hunts and eats other animals.

Wasp's wing mechanism

Proboscis
An insect's long, tubelike mouthparts. In some flies, the proboscis channels saliva to the surface of food. The semi-digested food is then sucked up through the proboscis.

Pupa
The inactive stage in some insects' life cycles in which they transform into adults. The pupa of a butterfly is called a chrysalis.

R

Resilin
A rubbery material found in insect wing-hinges and in pads at the base of a flea's back legs. Resilin stores and releases energy to enable a flea to jump.

Greenbottle fly

S

Sense receptors
Receptors on any part of an insect's head, body, or appendages that receive sensory stimuli, for example vibrations.

Setae
Hairs on an insect's head, body, or appendages. Setae are extensions of the exoskeleton, and many are sensitive.

Spiracles
Holes found along each side of an insect's body through which the insect takes in and expels air. The spiracles can be opened and closed to control the passage of air. The spiracles are connected to the tracheae (breathing tubes) inside the insect.

A single eyelet of the compound eye

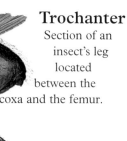

T

Thorax
The middle region of an insect's body. An insect's wings and legs are attached to the thorax.

Tracheae
Interconnecting breathing tubes throughout an insect's body. Air flows through the tubes, taking oxygen to the tissues. The tracheae are flexible so that they can expand and contract in order to take in and expel air through the spiracles.

Trochanter
Section of an insect's leg located between the coxa and the femur.

Index

Acknowledgements

Editorial assistance:
Julie Ferris and Nicki Waine

Design assistance:
Iain Morris and Jason Gonzalez

Additional photography:
Peter Chadwick, Gill Ellsbury,
Frank Greenaway and Neil Fletcher

Photoshop retouching:
Bob Warner and Oblong Box

Thanks to:
John Brackenbury for editorial
consultancy; Marion Dent for index

Illustrations:
12tr, 24cr, 25cr, 41tr Simone End; 23tr
Michael Lamb

Picture credits
r=right, l=left, c=centre, t=top, a=above,
b=below.

Ardea, London: John Clegg 17bc, JL
Mason 28tr; **Biofotos / Heather Angel**:
34bl; **John Brackenbury**: 11br, 18tr,
25br, 33bl, bc, 34tr; **Bruce Coleman
Collection**: Jane Burton 13tr, 40cr, c, cl,
41r, cl, John Cancalosi 2-3, 8c, 46-47,
Eric Crichton 14cr, MPL Fogden 11tr,
CB & DW Frith 27tr, Jeremy Grayson
36tr, Felix Labhardt 37tr, Andy Purcell
10bl, Dr Frieder Sauer 20br, Kim Taylor
front cover bc, 14tr, 20bc, 27br,
Carl Wallace 36bl, Peter Ward 13tl;
Microscopix: Andrew Syred 19br, 21tr,
tra, 22r, 23tc, cl, 24br, 40bl, br;
Natural History Museum, London:
6cl, 11c; **Natural History
Photographic Agency**: Anthony
Bannister 36cl, Stephen Dalton 13bl,
13br, Ron Fotheringham 30br, Peter
Parks 16br; **Oxford Scientific Films**:
GI Bernard 12bl, 14b, Michael Fogden
23b, David Fox 22bl, Avril Ramage
32br, James H Robinson 29bl, Kjell B
Sandved 22bc, Tim Sheperd 39bl;
Animals Animals: William D Griffin
25c, Raymond A Mendez 25tl;
Mantis Wildlife Films: Jim Frazier
31cr, br, **Photo Researchers Inc**:
Dawin Dale 20cl; **Planet Earth
Pictures**: Jon & Alison Moran 11bc;
Premaphotos Wildlife: KG Preston-
Mafham 10cra, 17cr, 24bl, 28cra, 37cr,
38b; **Science Photo Library**:
Dr Jeremy Burgess 14cl, 15br, 17br, 31l,
35cr, Dawin Dale front cover br, 20bl,
Manfred Kage 14clb, Alfred Pasieka
10br, JC Revy 30cl, 30cr, Dave Roberts
12br, spine, David Scharf 14c, 16cl,
38tr, 39br, Cath Wadforth 31tr;
Science Pictures Limited: 34cl.

Every effort has been made to trace
the copyright holders. Dorling
Kindersley apologises for any
unintentional omissions and would
be pleased, in such cases, to add an
acknowledgement in future editions.